This book is to be returned on or before
the last date

D0727210

NICK BUTTER

STORIE

Falkirk Council

To help people understand what God is like,
Jesus told lots of stories which are as exciting
today as when they were first heard.

The Precious Pearl is still a great favourite
and its message is one that children especially
love to hear.

Marshall Pickering
An Imprint of HarperCollins*Publishers*
77–85 Fulham Palace Road,
Hammersmith, London W6 8JB, UK
5 7 9 10 8 6 4

First published by Marshall Morgan & Scott in 1986
This edition published in 1994 by Marshall Pickering

A catalogue record for this book is available
from The British Library

0-551-02872-6

Printed in Hong Kong

The Precious Pearl

Nick Butterworth and Mick Inkpen

Marshall Pickering
An Imprint of HarperCollins*Publishers*

Here is a man who buys and
sells things.
He is called a merchant.
He has a fine fur coat and a
felt hat with a floppy feather.
It is his favourite.

The house he lives in is huge.
It has five floors and a fishpond
with a fountain in the front
garden.

The merchant has everything
he wants.
He has fifteen rooms filled
with furniture.

He has four freezers
full of food.
(And three fridges
for fizzy drinks.)

And there is more money under
his mattress than you could
ever imagine. Much more.
Yes, the merchant has everything
he wants, until...

One day, in a shop window, he sees something. Something special.
It is a wonderful white pearl.

'Five hundred thousand pounds,'
says the man in the shop.
It is even more money than the
merchant has under his mattress.
But he wants that pearl more
than anything in the world.

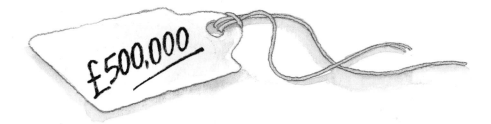

He hurries home. He has a plan.
He sells his furniture, his fridges
and his freezers full of food.
He sells his house, his fountain
and his fishpond.

He sells his fine fur coat.
But the felt hat with the
floppy feather, he keeps.
It is his favourite.

He borrows a barrow and
bundles in the money.
Off to the shop he trundles
to buy the pearl.

Oh dear! He is still six pounds short.

'Sell me your hat for six pounds,' says the man in the shop.

The merchant laughs.

He hands the man his hat and takes the pearl.

Hooray! The pearl is his at last.
Jesus says, 'God is like the
merchant's pearl.
It costs everything to know him.
But he is worth more than
anything in the world.'

You can read the story of **The Precious Pearl**
in Matthew chapter 13 verses 45 and 46.

Other titles in the **Stories Jesus Told** *series*
by Nick Butterworth and Mick Inkpen

The House On The Rock
The Lost Sheep
The Two Sons